The Altruist in Politics

Benjamin Cardozo

Contents

THE ALTRUIST IN POLITICS

BY

Benjamin Cardozo

"THE ALTRUIST IN POLITICS"
By Benjamin Cardozo

There comes not seldom a crisis in the life of men, of nations, and of worlds, when the old forms seem ready to decay, and the old rules of action have lost their binding force. The evils of existing systems obscure the blessings that attend them; and, where reform is needed, the cry is raised for subversion. The cause of such phenomena is not far to seek. "It used to appear to me," writes Count Tolstoi, in a significant passage, "it used to appear to me that the small number of cultivated, rich and idle men, of whom I was one, composed the whole of humanity, and that the millions and millions of other men who had lived and are still living were not in reality men at all." It is this spirit-the spirit that sees the whole of humanity in the few, and throws into the background the millions and millions of other men-it is this spirit that has aroused the antagonism of reformers, and made the decay of the old forms, the rupture of the old restrictions, the ideal of them and of their followers. When wealth and poverty meet each other face to face, the one the master and the other the dependent, the one exalted and the other debased, it is perhaps hardly matter for surprise that the dependent and debased and powerless faction, in envy of their opponents' supremacy, should demand, not simple reform, but absolute community and equality of wealth. That cry for communism is no new one in the history of mankind. Thousands of years ago it was heard and acted on; and, in the lapse of centuries, its reverberations have but swelled in volume. Again and again, the altruist has arisen in politics, has bidden us share with others the product of our toil, and has proclaimed the communistic dogma as the panacea for our social ills. So today, amid the buried hopes and buried projects of the past, the doctrine of communism still lives in the minds of men. Under stress of misfortune, or in dread of tyranny, it is still preached in modern times as Plato preached it in the world of the Greeks.

Yet it is indeed doubtful whether, in the history of mankind, a doctrine was ever taught more impracticable or more false to the principles it professes than this very doctrine of communism. In a world where self-interest is avowedly the ruling motive, it seeks to establish at once an all-reaching and all-controlling altruism. In a world where every man is pushing and fighting to outstrip his fellows, it would make him toil with like vigor for their common welfare. In a world where a man's activity is measured by the nearness of reward, it would hold up a prospective recompense as an equal stimulant to labor. "The more bitterly we feel," writes George Eliot, "the more bitterly we feel the folly, ignorance, neglect, or self-seeking of those who at different times have wielded power, the stronger is the obligation we lay on ourselves to beware lest we also, by a too hasty wresting of measures which seem to promise immediate relief, make a worse time of it for our own generation, and leave a bad inheritance for our children." In the future, when the remoteness of his reward shall have weakened the laborer's zeal, we shall be able to judge more fairly of the blessings that the communist offers. Instead of the present world, where some at least are well-to-do and happy, the communist holds before us a world where all alike are poor. For the activity, the push, the vigor of our modern life, his substitute is a life aimless and unbroken. And so we have to say to communists what George Eliot might have said: Be not blinded by the passions of the moment, but when you prate about your own wrongs and the sufferings of your offspring, take heed lest in the long run you make a worse time of it for your own generation, and leave a bad inheritance for your children.

Little thought has been taken by these altruistic reformers for the application of the doctrines they uphold. To the question how one kind of labor can be measured against another, how the labor of the artisan can be measured against the labor of the artist, how the labor of the strong can be measured against the labor of the weak, the communists can give no answer. Absorbed, as they are, in the principle of equality, they have still forgotten the equality of work in the equality of pay; they have forgotten that reward, to be really equal, must be proportionate to effort; and they and all socialists have forgotten that we cannot make an arithmetic of human thought and feeling; and that for all our crude attempts to balance recompense against toil, for all our crude attempts to determine the relative severity of different kinds of toil, for all our crude attempts to determine the relative strain on different persons of the same kind of toil, yet not only will the ratio, dealing, as it does, with our subjective feelings, be a blundering one, but a system based upon it will involve inequalities greater, because more insidious, than those of the present system it would discard.

Instances, indeed, are not wanting to substantiate the claim that communism, by unduly exalting our altruistic impulses, proceeds upon a false psychological basis. Yet if an instance is to be chosen, it would be hard to find one more suggestive than that afforded by the efforts of Robert Owen. The year 1824 saw the rise of Owen's little community of New Harmony, and the year of 1828 saw the community's final disruption. Individuals had appropriated to themselves the property designed for all; and even Owen, who had given to the enterprise his money and his life, was obliged to admit that men were not yet fitted for the communistic stage, and that the moment of transition from individualism to communism had not yet arrived. Men trained under the old system, with its eager rivalry, its selfish interests, could not quite yet enter into the spirit of self-renunciation that communism demands. And Owen, therefore, was led to put his trust in education as the great moulder of the minds of men. Through this agency, he hoped, the eager rivalry, the selfish interests, the sordid love of gain, might be lost in higher, purer, more disinterested ends; and, animated by that hope-the hope that in the fullness of time another New Harmony, free from contention and the disappointments of the old one, might serve to immortalize his name-animated by that hope, Owen passed the last thirty years of his life; and with that hope still before his eyes he died.

But years now have passed since Owen lived; the second New Harmony has not yet been seen; the so-called rational system of education has not yet transformed the impulses or the aims of men; and the communist of today, with a history of two thousand years of failure behind him, in the same pathetic confidence still looks for the realization of his dreams to the communism of the future.

And yet, granting that communism were practicable, granting that Owen's hopes had some prospect of fulfillment, the doctrine still embodies evils that must make it forever inexpedient. The readers of Mr. Matthew Arnold's works must have noticed the emphasis with which he dwells on the instinct of expansion as a factor in human progress. It is the refutation alike of communism and socialism that they thwart the instinct of expansion; that they substitute for individual energy the energy of the government; that they substitute for human personality the blind, mechanical power of the State. The one system, as the other, marks the end of individualism. The one system, as the other, would make each man the image of his neighbor. The one system, as the other, would hold back the progressive, and, by uniformity of reward, gain uniformity of type.

I can look forward to no blissful prospect for a race of men that, under the dominion of the State, at the cost of all freedom of action, at the cost, indeed, of their own true selves, shall enjoy, if one will, a fair abundance of the material blessings of life. Some Matthew Arnold of the future would inevitably say of them in phase like that applied to the Puritans of old: "They entered the prison of socialism and had the key turned upon their spirit there for hundreds of years." Into that prison of socialism, with broken enterprise and broken energy, as serfs under the mastery of the State, while human personality is preferred to unreasoning mechanism, mankind must hesitate to step. When they shall once have entered within it, when the key shall have been turned upon their spirit and have confined them in narrower straits than even Puritanism could have done, it will be left for them to find, in their blind obedience and passive submission, the recompense for the singleness of character, the foresight, and the energy, that they have left behind them.

In almost every phase of life, this doctrine of political altruists is equally impracticable and pernicious. In its social results, it involves the substitution of the community in the family's present position. In its political aspects, it involves the absolute dominion of the

State over the actions and property of its subjects. Thus, though claiming to be an exaltation of the so-called natural rights of liberty and equality, it is in reality their emphatic debasement. It teaches that thoughtless docility is a recompense for stunted enterprise. It magnifies material good at the cost of every rational endowment. It inculcates a self-denial that must result in dwarfing the individual to a mere instrument in the hands of the State for the benefit of his fellows. No such organization of society-no organization that fails to take note of the fact that man must have scope for the exercise and development of his faculties-no such organization of society can ever reach a permanent success. However beneficent its motives, the hypothesis with which it starts can never be realized. The aphorism of Emerson, "Churches have been built, not upon principles, but upon tropes," is as true in the field of politics as it is in the field of religion. In a like figurative spirit, the followers of communism have reared their edifice; and, looking back upon the finished structure, seeking to discern the base on which it rests, the critic finds, not principles, but tropes. The builders have appealed to a future that has no warrant in the past; and fixing their gaze upon the distant dreamland, captivated by the vision there beheld, entranced by its ideal effulgence, their eyes were blinded to the real conditions of the human problem they had set before them. Their enemies have not been slow to note such weakness and mistake; and perhaps it may serve to clear up misconceptions, perhaps it may serve to lessen cant and open the way for fresh and vigorous thought, if we shall once convince ourselves that altruism cannot be the rule of life; that its logical result is the dwarfing of the individual man; and that not by the death of human personality can we hope to banish the evils of our day, and to realize the ideal of all existence, a nobler or purer life.

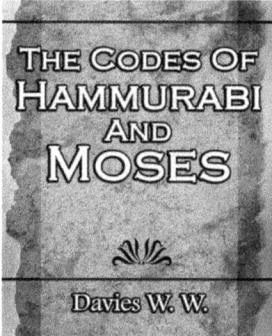

The Codes Of Hammurabi And Moses
W. W. Davies

QTY

The discovery of the Hammurabi Code is one of the greatest achievements of archaeology, and is of paramount interest, not only to the student of the Bible, but also to all those interested in ancient history...

Religion   ISBN: *1-59462-338-4*   Pages:132
MSRP $12.95

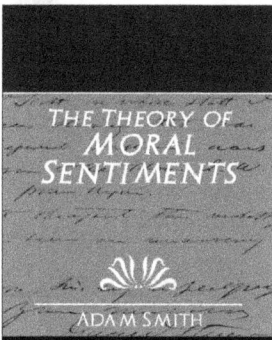

The Theory of Moral Sentiments
Adam Smith

QTY

This work from 1749. contains original theories of conscience amd moral judgment and it is the foundation for systemof morals.

Philosophy ISBN: *1-59462-777-0*   Pages:536
MSRP $19.95

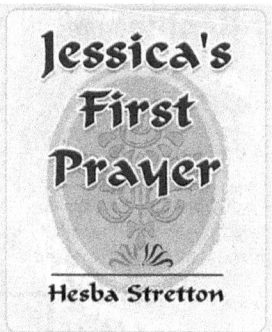

Jessica's First Prayer
Hesba Stretton

QTY

In a screened and secluded corner of one of the many railway-bridges which span the streets of London there could be seen a few years ago, from five o'clock every morning until half past eight, a tidily set-out coffee-stall, consisting of a trestle and board, upon which stood two large tin cans, with a small fire of charcoal burning under each so as to keep the coffee boiling during the early hours of the morning when the work-people were thronging into the city on their way to their daily toil...

Pages:84

Childrens   ISBN: *1-59462-373-2*   *MSRP $9.95*

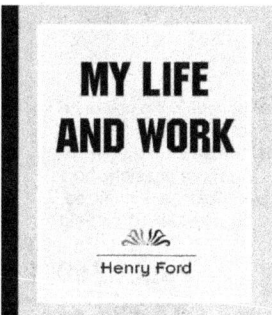

My Life and Work
Henry Ford

QTY

Henry Ford revolutionized the world with his implementation of mass production for the Model T automobile. Gain valuable business insight into his life and work with his own auto-biography... "We have only started on our development of our country we have not as yet, with all our talk of wonderful progress, done more than scratch the surface. The progress has been wonderful enough but..."

Pages:300

Biographies/   ISBN: *1-59462-198-5*   *MSRP $21.95*

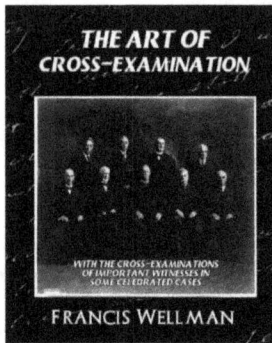

The Art of Cross-Examination
Francis Wellman

QTY

I presume it is the experience of every author, after his first book is published upon an important subject, to be almost overwhelmed with a wealth of ideas and illustrations which could readily have been included in his book, and which to his own mind, at least, seem to make a second edition inevitable. Such certainly was the case with me; and when the first edition had reached its sixth impression in five months, I rejoiced to learn that it seemed to my publishers that the book had met with a sufficiently favorable reception to justify a second and considerably enlarged edition. ..

Pages:412

Reference   ISBN: *1-59462-647-2*   *MSRP $19.95*

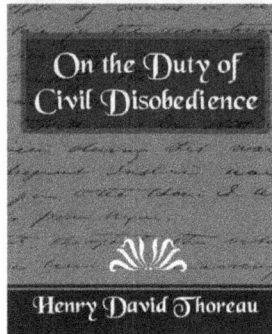

On the Duty of Civil Disobedience
Henry David Thoreau

QTY

Thoreau wrote his famous essay, On the Duty of Civil Disobedience, as a protest against an unjust but popular war and the immoral but popular institution of slave-owning. He did more than write—he declined to pay his taxes, and was hauled off to gaol in consequence. Who can say how much this refusal of his hastened the end of the war and of slavery ?

Law   ISBN: *1-59462-747-9*   **Pages:48**

MSRP $7.45

Dream Psychology Psychoanalysis for Beginners
Sigmund Freud

QTY

Sigmund Freud, born Sigismund Schlomo Freud (May 6, 1856 - September 23, 1939), was a Jewish-Austrian neurologist and psychiatrist who co-founded the psychoanalytic school of psychology. Freud is best known for his theories of the unconscious mind, especially involving the mechanism of repression; his redefinition of sexual desire as mobile and directed towards a wide variety of objects; and his therapeutic techniques, especially his understanding of transference in the therapeutic relationship and the presumed value of dreams as sources of insight into unconscious desires.

Pages:196

Psychology   ISBN: *1-59462-905-6*   *MSRP $15.45*

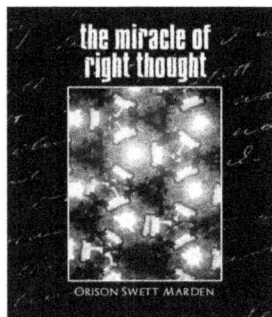

The Miracle of Right Thought
Orison Swett Marden

QTY

Believe with all of your heart that you will do what you were made to do. When the mind has once formed the habit of holding cheerful, happy, prosperous pictures, it will not be easy to form the opposite habit. It does not matter how improbable or how far away this realization may see, or how dark the prospects may be, if we visualize them as best we can, as vividly as possible, hold tenaciously to them and vigorously struggle to attain them, they will gradually become actualized, realized in the life. But a desire, a longing without endeavor, a yearning abandoned or held indifferently will vanish without realization.

Pages:360

Self Help   ISBN: *1-59462-644-8*   *MSRP $25.45*

www.bookjungle.com *email: sales@bookjungle.com fax: 630-214-0564 mail: Book Jungle PO Box 2226 Champaign, IL 61825*

QTY

The Rosicrucian Cosmo-Conception Mystic Christianity *by Max Heindel*   ISBN: *1-59462-188-8* **$38.95**
The Rosicrucian Cosmo-conception is not dogmatic, neither does it appeal to any other authority than the reason of the student. It is: not controversial, but is: sent forth in the, hope that it may help to clear...   New Age/Religion Pages 646

Abandonment To Divine Providence *by Jean-Pierre de Caussade*   ISBN: *1-59462-228-0* **$25.95**
"The Rev. Jean Pierre de Caussade was one of the most remarkable spiritual writers of the Society of Jesus in France in the 18th Century. His death took place at Toulouse in 1751. His works have gone through many editions and have been republished...   Inspirational/Religion Pages 400

Mental Chemistry *by Charles Haanel*   ISBN: *1-59462-192-6* **$23.95**
Mental Chemistry allows the change of material conditions by combining and appropriately utilizing the power of the mind. Much like applied chemistry creates something new and unique out of careful combinations of chemicals the mastery of mental chemistry...   New Age Pages 354

The Letters of Robert Browning and Elizabeth Barret Barrett 1845-1846 vol II   ISBN: *1-59462-193-4* **$35.95**
by Robert Browning and Elizabeth Barrett   Biographies Pages 596

Gleanings In Genesis (volume I) *by Arthur W. Pink*   ISBN: *1-59462-130-6* **$27.45**
Appropriately has Genesis been termed "the seed plot of the Bible" for in it we have, in germ form, almost all of the great doctrines which are afterwards fully developed in the books of Scripture which follow...   Religion/Inspirational Pages 420

The Master Key *by L. W. de Laurence*   ISBN: *1-59462-001-6* **$30.95**
In no branch of human knowledge has there been a more lively increase of the spirit of research during the past few years than in the study of Psychology, Concentration and Mental Discipline. The requests for authentic lessons in Thought Control, Mental Discipline and...   New Age/Business Pages 422

The Lesser Key Of Solomon Goetia *by L. W. de Laurence*   ISBN: *1-59462-092-X* **$9.95**
This translation of the first book of the "Lernegton" which is now for the first time made accessible to students of Talismanic Magic was done, after careful collation and edition, from numerous Ancient Manuscripts in Hebrew, Latin, and French...   New Age/Occult Pages 92

Rubaiyat Of Omar Khayyam *by Edward Fitzgerald*   ISBN: *1-59462-332-5* **$13.95**
Edward Fitzgerald, whom the world has already learned, in spite of his own efforts to remain within the shadow of anonymity, to look upon as one of the rarest poets of the century, was born at Bredfield, in Suffolk, on the 31st of March, 1809. He was the third son of John Purcell...   Music Pages 172

Ancient Law *by Henry Maine*   ISBN: *1-59462-128-4* **$29.95**
The chief object of the following pages is to indicate some of the earliest ideas of mankind, as they are reflected in Ancient Law, and to point out the relation of those ideas to modern thought.   Religion/History Pages 452

Far-Away Stories *by William J. Locke*   ISBN: *1-59462-129-2* **$19.45**
"Good wine needs no bush, but a collection of mixed vintages does. And this book is just such a collection. Some of the stories I do not want to remain buried for ever in the museum files of dead magazine-numbers an author's not unpardonable vanity..."   Fiction Pages 272

Life of David Crockett *by David Crockett*   ISBN: *1-59462-250-7* **$27.45**
"Colonel David Crockett was one of the most remarkable men of the times in which he lived. Born in humble life, but gifted with a strong will, an indomitable courage, and unremitting perseverance...   Biographies/New Age Pages 424

Lip-Reading *by Edward Nitchie*   ISBN: *1-59462-206-X* **$25.95**
Edward B. Nitchie, founder of the New York School for the Hard of Hearing, now the Nitchie School of Lip-Reading, Inc, wrote "LIP-READING Principles and Practice". The development and perfecting of this meritorious work on lip-reading was an undertaking...   How-to Pages 400

A Handbook of Suggestive Therapeutics, Applied Hypnotism, Psychic Science   ISBN: *1-59462-214-0* **$24.95**
by Henry Munro   Health/New Age/Health/Self-help Pages 376

A Doll's House: and Two Other Plays *by Henrik Ibsen*   ISBN: *1-59462-112-8* **$19.95**
Henrik Ibsen created this classic when in revolutionary 1848 Rome. Introducing some striking concepts in playwriting for the realist genre, this play has been studied the world over.   Fiction/Classics/Plays 308

The Light of Asia *by sir Edwin Arnold*   ISBN: *1-59462-204-3* **$13.95**
In this poetic masterpiece, Edwin Arnold describes the life and teachings of Buddha. The man who was to become known as Buddha to the world was born as Prince Gautama of India but he rejected the worldly riches and abandoned the reigns of power when...   Religion/History/Biographies Pages 170

The Complete Works of Guy de Maupassant *by Guy de Maupassant*   ISBN: *1-59462-157-8* **$16.95**
"For days and days, nights and nights, I had dreamed of that first kiss which was to consecrate our engagement, and I knew not on what spot I should put my lips..."   Fiction/Classics Pages 240

The Art of Cross-Examination *by Francis L. Wellman*   ISBN: *1-59462-309-0* **$26.95**
Written by a renowned trial lawyer, Wellman imparts his experience and uses case studies to explain how to use psychology to extract desired information through questioning.   How-to/Science/Reference Pages 408

Answered or Unanswered? *by Louisa Vaughan*   ISBN: *1-59462-248-5* **$10.95**
Miracles of Faith in China   Religion Pages 112

The Edinburgh Lectures on Mental Science (1909) *by Thomas*   ISBN: *1-59462-008-3* **$11.95**
This book contains the substance of a course of lectures recently given by the writer in the Queen Street Hail, Edinburgh. Its purpose is to indicate the Natural Principles governing the relation between Mental Action and Material Conditions...   New Age/Psychology Pages 148

Ayesha *by H. Rider Haggard*   ISBN: *1-59462-301-5* **$24.95**
Verily and indeed it is the unexpected that happens! Probably if there was one person upon the earth from whom the Editor of this, and of a certain previous history, did not expect to hear again...   Classics Pages 380

Ayala's Angel *by Anthony Trollope*   ISBN: *1-59462-352-X* **$29.95**
The two girls were both pretty, but Lucy who was twenty-one who supposed to be simple and comparatively unattractive, whereas Ayala was credited, as her Bombwhat romantic name might show, with poetic charm and a taste for romance. Ayala when her father died was nineteen...   Fiction Pages 484

The American Commonwealth *by James Bryce*   ISBN: *1-59462-286-8* **$34.45**
An interpretation of American democratic political theory. It examines political mechanics and society from the perspective of Scotsman James Bryce   Politics Pages 572

Stories of the Pilgrims *by Margaret P. Pumphrey*   ISBN: *1-59462-116-0* **$17.95**
This book explores pilgrims religious oppression in England as well as their escape to Holland and eventual crossing to America on the Mayflower, and their early days in New England...   History Pages 268

www.bookjungle.com *email: sales@bookjungle.com fax: 630-214-0564 mail: Book Jungle PO Box 2226 Champaign, IL 61825*

QTY

The Fasting Cure *by Sinclair Upton*   ISBN: *1-59462-222-1* **$13.95**
In the Cosmopolitan Magazine for May, 1910, and in the Contemporary Review (London) for April, 1910, I published an article dealing with my experiences in fasting. I have written a great many magazine articles, but never one which attracted so much attention... New Age/Self Help/Health Pages 164

Hebrew Astrology *by Sepharial*   ISBN: *1-59462-308-2* **$13.45**
In these days of advanced thinking it is a matter of common observation that we have left many of the old landmarks behind and that we are now pressing forward to greater heights and to a wider horizon than that which represented the mind-content of our progenitors... Astrology Pages 144

Thought Vibration or The Law of Attraction in the Thought World   ISBN: *1-59462-127-6* **$12.95**
by William Walker Atkinson   Psychology/Religion Pages 144

Optimism *by Helen Keller*   ISBN: *1-59462-108-X* **$15.95**
Helen Keller was blind, deaf, and mute since 19 months old, yet famously learned how to overcome these handicaps, communicate with the world, and spread her lectures promoting optimism. An inspiring read for everyone... Biographies/Inspirational Pages 84

Sara Crewe *by Frances Burnett*   ISBN: *1-59462-360-0* **$9.45**
In the first place, Miss Minchin lived in London. Her home was a large, dull, tall one, in a large, dull square, where all the houses were alike, and all the sparrows were alike, and where all the door-knockers made the same heavy sound... Childrens/Classic Pages 88

The Autobiography of Benjamin Franklin *by Benjamin Franklin*   ISBN: *1-59462-135-7* **$24.95**
The Autobiography of Benjamin Franklin has probably been more extensively read than any other American historical work, and no other book of its kind has had such ups and downs of fortune. Franklin lived for many years in England, where he was agent... Biographies/History Pages 332

Name	
Email	
Telephone	
Address	
City, State ZIP	

☐ **Credit Card**   ☐ **Check / Money Order**

Credit Card Number	
Expiration Date	
Signature	

Please Mail to: Book Jungle
PO Box 2226
Champaign, IL 61825
or Fax to: 630-214-0564

ORDERING INFORMATION
web*: www.bookjungle.com*
email*: sales@bookjungle.com*
fax*: 630-214-0564*
mail*: Book Jungle PO Box 2226 Champaign, IL 61825*
or PayPal *to sales@bookjungle.com*

Please contact us for bulk discounts

DIRECT-ORDER TERMS

20% Discount if You Order Two or More Books
Free Domestic Shipping!
Accepted: Master Card, Visa, Discover, American Express

www.ingramcontent.com/pod-product-compliance
Lightning Source LLC
Chambersburg PA
CBHW081242090426
42738CB00016B/3375